An Itchy Round Rash

By

Dr. Farah Alam-Mirza, MRCGP, DCH, DRCOG, DFSRH, PG Certificate in Teaching

Illustrations by Yunzila Mirza

Copyright Dr. F. Alam-Mirza

"Hello, Mum. Are we going to the soft play area today?" asked Toby, as Mum came to pick him up from school.

"Yes we are, let's go," replied Mum.

"Hurray for soft play!" cried Toby, as he hurried towards the ball pit.

"Hi, Toby!" called Zane. "Let's play!"

"Hi, Zane!" cried Toby, as they began to play.

"What's that?" asked Toby, pointing to a round red mark on Zane's arm. "Do you have a tattoo?"

"I don't know what it is," said Zane.

Later on, Mum came to pick Toby up.

"Come on, Toby, time to go home," called Mum. "Did you have a nice time?"

"Yes, it was great fun!" replied Toby. "When can I come here again?"

"Soon," said Mum.

"Bye, Zane! See you next time!" called Toby.

"See you!" said Zane.

A few days later, Toby was scratching his arm a lot.

"Are you all right, Toby?" asked Mum.

"My arm is so itchy!" replied Toby.

"Let's see," said Mum.

Toby had a round red rash on his arm.

"How did you get that?" asked Mum.

"I don't know," said Toby.

"Did you hurt yourself?"

"No, I didn't. Zane has it, too," replied Toby.

"Oh dear, we had better get it checked by the doctor," said Mum.

"How are you today, Toby?" asked Dr. Alam.

"I'm good, thank you," replied Toby. "I have this funny mark on my arm."

"This is ringworm," said Dr. Alam.

"How did he get it?" asked Mum, anxiously. "Toby has never had this before!"

"It is a fungal infection caught by touching someone else who has the rash," said Dr. Alam.

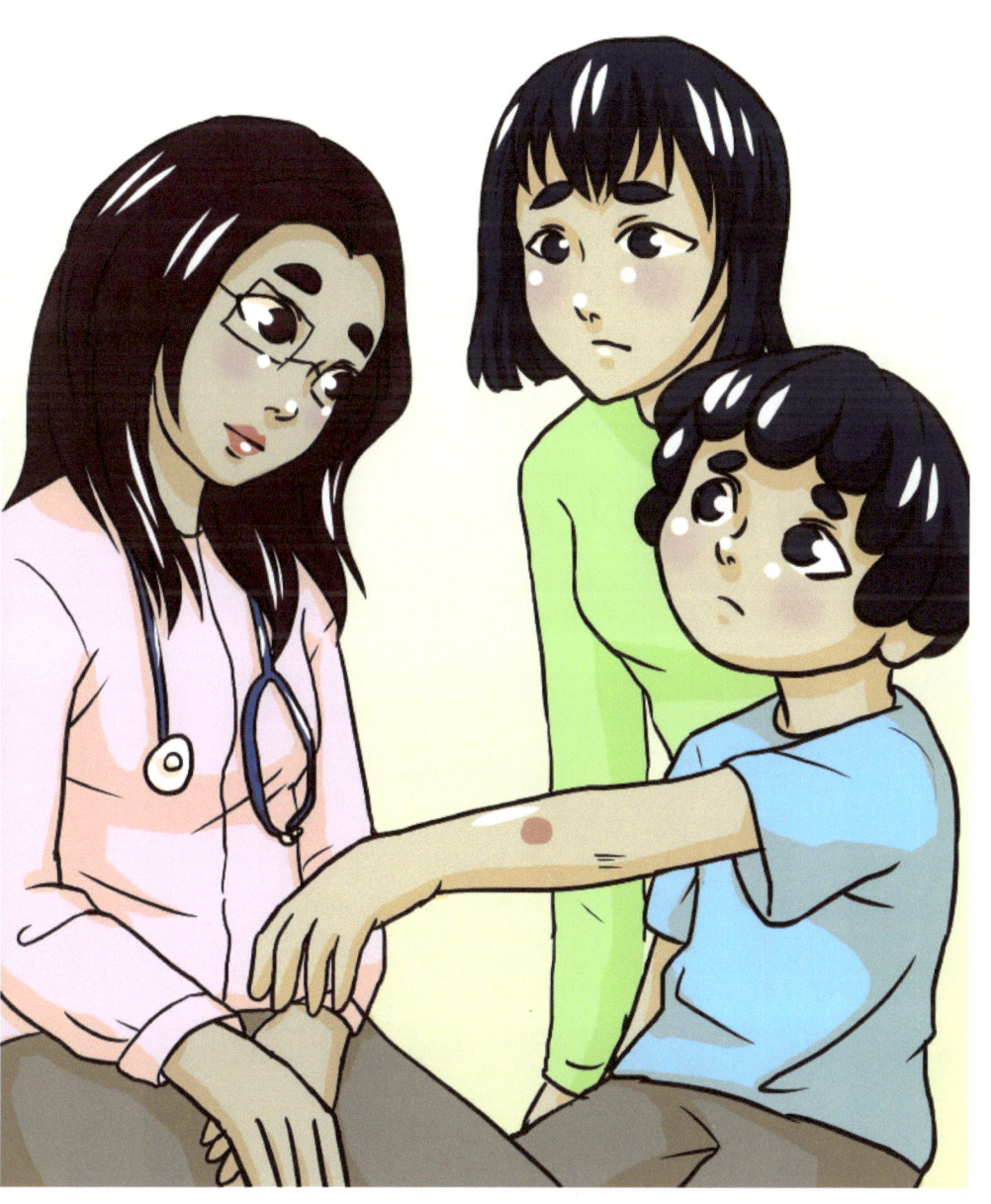

"Zane has it, too. I saw it when we were at soft play!" exclaimed Toby. "Uh oh! Did I get it from him?"

"You probably did," said Mum.

"It is called ringworm, because it usually comes up in red round patches, which are itchy. You catch the germs from other people."

"I will give you an antibiotic cream to use. Be careful to avoid sharing towels and clothes while it is there, to prevent it from spreading to others," explained Dr. Alam.

"Continue the cream for ten days after the rash has gone, otherwise it can come back from the deeper layers of the skin."

Toby was scratching his arm.

"Try not to scratch it," said Dr. Alam, "and wash your hands after touching it. Otherwise, it can spread to other areas on your body!"

"I won't touch it now!" said Toby.

Later on Mum put the cream on for Toby.

"There, this will make it all better," she said. "It's almost bed-time. Are you ready to brush your teeth?"

"Not yet, Mum. I need my own towel first!" said Toby.

"Well done!" said Mum.

Questions

1. What germ causes an itchy round rash?

2. How do you catch an itchy round rash?

3. How can you avoid spreading a fungal infection?

Answers

1. Fungus

2. By touching someone who has the rash

3. Avoid sharing towels and clothes, and wash your hands after touching the rash.

About this book

The aim of this series is to promote awareness and wellbeing in children, to prevent disease and illness, and to encourage a healthy lifestyle in a fun and interactive way.

Disclaimer

This book is for educational purposes only. It is not meant to be a substitute for professional medical advice. Always seek the advice of your doctor if you are unwell.

Health Promotion Series

Available on Amazon:

"Wash Your Hands"

"Ouch, I Need a Plaster!"

"Drink Up"

"Achoo!"

"5 a-Day, Every day"

"Brush Your Teeth"

"Sunkissed"

"Worms Away"

www.ingramcontent.com/pod-product-compliance
Lightning Source LLC
Chambersburg PA
CBHW041809040426
42449CB00001B/25